Luminous Other

Luminous Other

Poems

Robin Davidson

THE ASHLAND POETRY PRESS

Printed in the United States of America

ISBN: 978-0-912592-75-6

Library of Congress Control Number: 2013940035

Cover art: Stained glass window designed by Stanisław Wyspiański and located in the Basilica of St. Francis of Assisi, Kraków, Poland. Cover photo is used by permission of the Franciscan Fathers.

Cover design: Nicholas Fedorchak

Author photo: Tony Davidson

This book has been funded in part by the Houston Arts Alliance Individual Artist Grant Program (2009).

Acknowledgments

Acknowledgment is made to the editors of the following journals in which these poems, some in slightly different versions, first appeared:

Fraza, "Braiding" ("Zaplatanie warkoczy"), "In An Amsterdam Hotel"("W jednym z hoteli w Amsterdamie"), and "What Mrs. Schmetterling Wants" ("Czego pragnie pani Schmetterling"), Polish translations by Ewa Elżbieta Nowakowska. (*Fraza* is a Polish literary journal published in Rzeszów, Poland.)

Paris Review, "Women Harvesting: Virgins, Widows, Wives"

Poet Lore, "Braiding"

qarrtsiluni, "April Storm" and "August Garden"

Tampa Review, "Religion by Design," "Revisions," "Window," and "The Angel of Architecture"

Texas Review, "The Reader"

"The Angel of Architecture," "Religion by Design," and "The Rothko Chapel, Houston, Early Spring" were reprinted in *Improbable Worlds: an Anthology of Texas and Louisiana Poets*.

The "Mrs. Schmetterling" poems comprise a poem cycle dedicated to Polish poet Ewa Lipska and published by Calypso Editions as part of the chapbook, *City that Ripens on the Tree of the World*.

I am grateful to the Houston Arts Alliance for a 2009 New Works Fellowship in Literature awarded through the Individual Artist Grant Program, and to the University of Houston-Downtown for a 2012 Faculty Development Leave Award, for their support in the development of these poems.

My deepest thanks also go to poets Edward Hirsch, Martha Serpas, Elizabeth Spires, Susan Wood and Adam Zagajewski for their faith in my work, and to Deborah Fleming, Sarah Wells and the Ashland Poetry Press for their generosity in the crafting of this book.

For my beloveds
Tony, Joshua, and Chelsea

Contents

III. If Grief Were a Bird

...and leave you (inexpressibly to untangle)
your life afraid and huge and ripening,
so that it, now bound in and now embracing,
grows alternately stone in you and star.

—Rainer Maria Rilke

"Evening," The Book of Images
Translated by Edward Snow

Postcolonial Eve

After a photograph by Margo Ovcharenko, Moscow

Face half-hidden in shadow,
        torso, breast, arms, knee
                intertwined, a delicate foliage of flesh—
she is a tree of
        secrets and revelations,
                what burns and what turns to ash.
She does not want history. She does not need
        to know the sequence of changing vowels in the name
                of a city. She is
a body free of forgiveness.
        The room is a garden.
In her, light ripens.

I

City that Ripens
on the Tree
of the World

An Ascension

After a photograph by Daria Tuminas, St. Petersburg

I.

What we see first are the feet, a woman suspended
in midair from the unseen—whether rafter or rope
or branch of an invisible tree—
then the toenails polished green as leaves
in the hem of her floral dress.
The gazer's eye moves on, among coat and chair,
shawl and blanket, the open cigarette pack,
matches, ashtray, the last palpable newsprint
she will hold in her invisible hands. All of this
rests on the floor's rough-hewn wood—
like an ancient tree flayed and stretched beneath her.
And so we assume the worst:
A woman steps from the chair's edge to hang herself
like a dress in the room's close dark.

II.

In the middle of his own life's path, Dante
began to write his way out of exile.
He needed saving from his own rage. An inferno
turned ascension that he would name
poetry, then love, then mystical sainthood.
He invented the *Wood of the Suicides* as reminder:
Those who take their own lives lose the right
to live again in human form. Dante believed
he must follow the call of the Rood,
not the shrill cry of snapped branches,

the tormented soul speaking. He must leave
the domain of poets in order to ascend.
No empathy among the angels.

III.

In the essay Yeats called "Magic," Eden
is a walled garden on a mountain summit two miles
high. And from the garden's center the Tree
of Knowledge rises. In its branches the birds build
their nests, and angels stand among them.
And this same tree is the Tree of Life
where sighing souls move in its branches
instead of sap, whose apples bear human faces,
and if you placed your ear close enough,
you could hear within the tree's fruit
the struggle of voices trapped in an inner dark.

IV.

Dante and Yeats believed in other worlds, in the tree
as emissary for creation's complex paradox—
but the woman here, whose feet reveal her,
believes only in the reach for light,
follows the call of the simple tree
growing in her mind. First, green figs,
then a weightlessness and a rising.
Her entire body afloat in the night sky, ascending.

Mrs. Schmetterling Kneels in a Garden

For Ewa Lipska

Mrs. Schmetterling, let's call her Judith, married.
She is neither great musician nor poet.
Not scientist nor historian. She is ordinary.
Any century's woman. She cooks, reads, bathes children
and dogs. She takes out the garbage, listens to music.
Mrs. Schmetterling is tired. Her imagination is
pressed like a tiny chestnut blossom between the pages
of old letters and recipes, a book of days.
She would like to give herself advice, chide herself not
to remain invisible, feeding on the erotic bread
of great art. But she doesn't. She hesitates, keeps herself
at arm's length. A practice she learned from her mother.
Instead she kneels in a garden, breaks open
each amaryllis pod in her palm, peels back
the green triangles of skin forming the bolus
left from the blossom and sprinkles
the black ash of seedlings onto the clay.

The Reader

What she could not say herself, she looked for
in the voices of other women.
Between the black and white lines of words,
the books lining cherrywood shelves spoke,
and she listened. But she longed for her own
visible voice rising
out of dark wood and paper, flying.
Her mother had been a painter, so silent,
she learned to study the shoulders, the small hands,
the large veins cerulean blue rising like water in her skin,
for a sign, a music, the rhythm of a voice
she believed waited, but
it was her father who read to her,
and she swallowed his voice,
listened and listened, hungry for language
until he lived in her, his silent daughter,
a girl knitting songbirds between her eyebrows,
painting flight on her tongue.

If I could find her now, that girl made of fathers
and books, I would open the fist in her throat,
the way a magician releases unseen doves from his palm,
and offer her the imagistic world:
Lavender blossoms swelling on the magnolia tree's
bare limbs just outside her window,
the flowering before the foliage.
Church bells at noon,
red and yellow tulips leaning into a city street.
Park pigeons purling, awash in rusts and greens.
A swimmer's shoulders, oar-like arms,

slicing into salt water, wave-froth,
a dawn-red sea.
And I would challenge her
to know these with her own bare skin.

City that Ripens on the Tree of the World

The tree outside Mrs. Schmetterling's flat
is a cathedral. Its black branches are stones

luminous with ice windows.
The tree's single chorister's a black and white magpie

whose visible grace is a persistent scavenging.
She knows such scavenging.

She loves this bird.
Mrs. Schmetterling watches the November

seasonal seam open to a dual harvest.
She lives at an intersection

where Krupnicza Street crosses Mickiewicz Avenue,
where barley and the great Romantic poet collide.

When night falls, Mrs. Schmetterling will see
two moons rise outside her window,

like laundry hung out piece by piece
over a balcony in winter wind. One pure, bright,

the original moon. The other, its shadow
or some odd reflection caught

on the outside of the glass in the branches. No,
they hang in the inner lace of curtains along her desk,

so that she stands, takes the lace in her hands,
turns it to the left, the right.

But this doubleness stays.
Twin sisters of half-light, side by side,

hovering above her. If only one of them turned,
the moon would be full.

Window

It is my first afternoon in Kraków. At the back of the Franciscan Church,
I see the Wyspiański window where God creates the world
with a single stroke. Hair, body swirling, fluid
like the robes of a wizard, he is a flying mane, a glass hand—
upraised, poised for touch but suspended there, throbbing—
the October Polish sun for a moment flooding the room.

In the photograph it is 1978. My father stands in the kitchen
of my grandmother's old house on Ruby Drive.
In his left hand he holds a glass of scotch. His right is raised above his head,
fingers outstretched as if to wave to the camera, or bless the others.
He is drunk with the presence of all he loves
gathered in a single room.

This is when I first know our world is a window:
Porous realm of what is or was or could be.

Dusk in Jordan Park

ul. Ingardena, Kraków
For Adam Zagajewski

The shoulders of the poets are covered with snow.
Their eye sockets are lined with ice.
Even the composer is silent, each circle and staff of
his mind's music frozen flat in a field of white.

I move my ungloved hand along these old half-figures,
      trace each name twice—
            Mickiewicz, Słowacki, Chopin, Kochanowski—

Stone ghosts, I ask you,
are you human treasure wrenched from ruin and kept?
Are you home in the clay which holds you?
Or do you long to walk, as I do,
ordinary among the living

slang of streets, deformed noses of the old drunks,
the hollyhocks and mud lathering the hollow of old lap
of the *pani* whose skirts brush my ankles
when she asks me my first name?

I continue my circular walk, watch the slow snow
fall like stars forming behind the eyes
as if a chronic migraine had begun, as relentless
as history's pulse
until all paths of this labyrinthine garden,

            pruned shrubs, wooden benches, towering pines,
        are powdered with a rose-white-light-going-blue.

Św. Maria Magdalena Pisząca

Saint Mary Magdalene Writing
by the Master of the Female Half-Figures (Antwerp)
Czartoryski Museum, Kraków

In the first half of the sixteenth century the painter resurrects her,
dresses her not as the Jewess mourning her dead lover
but as Christian noblewoman, the Renaissance crimson of her bust line
half-hidden in black velvet sleeves which open first onto forearms—
cuffed in lace, each layer banded by ribbon, its gilt embroidery—
and then onto wrists, elongated fingers, the poised quill.

　　　　She is in the mind of the man who makes her a woman forgiven
of poverty, passion, her first profession.
Her head is covered, bowed to the page,
fifteen hundred years of letters or poems or prayers
accumulating in her hands.

She is alone, composed and composing. No god's voice
asks—*woman, why are you weeping?*—her reverie, a painted peace
assumed by a man whose hands believe in sainthood.
He has given her comforts—coffee urn, ink well, the desk's smooth surface.
As proof of lyric time or of eternity, he has hung
a clock behind her—its red face reads 8:40, morning, a winter sun.

　　　　This writing is her first task, whether joy or torment,
and she opens all of her body to it so that morning light
moves through her as if she were window grating or gauze or porous soul.
She must be cold, so much of her shoulders exposed.
She must be tired, sitting so long.

The Star: A Tarot Card

She kneels naked in what might be Eden,
balances her weight between two landscapes,
one knee bent, a genuflection
in the grass, the other raised
as she leans, extends her foot into
the garden pool.
The slope of ground almost forgotten,
she thinks of her hands,
these pitchers, full as breasts,
which spill their liquid deep into the grass,
cut rivulets like roads,
paths which turn,
wander, arrive by wandering.

Who paints her young Egyptian flesh so white
that it burns in starlight?
What wizard's will keeps her
under the eight-pointed star
like the spokes of the Great Wheel
which turns upon itself?
What must she gather out of the silence
to rise, go from this green place
alone, no man to name or take her,
no snake among the apples,
only the scarlet ibis
perched like a thought, a hunger
in the distant tree?

The Tree in the Library

I dreamt I lived one summer
in your library
where the walls were hung with books
and O'Keeffe's paintings of apples.
Mornings I'd reach for the shelves,
gather what I could,
then sit on the couch by your desk
and take into myself
sun on apples and a book.

Afternoons I'd nap, dream the body of a woman
part by part, in photographs
as Stieglitz dreamt O'Keeffe,
and each day the apples inside me
grew larger, like human faces waiting
for a voice, and the apples on the wall
began to swell, filling the room, opening
like skin unfolded, torn
to find the same woman
dreamt again and again,
each book singing its own fruit.

Double Paradise

Two paradises 'twere in one
To live in paradise alone.
—Andrew Marvell

He sought a double paradise, to be alone
with his own green thought, and she

kept a garden of her own where she knelt
on terra cotta tiles, dug until her fingers

bled, until she wore the black churning
of sticks and roots and clay beneath her nails.

He was at home in libraries and the anonymity
of fast food restaurants, moved between these

as a man bereft paces the shore of a river
he cannot cross, while she made a wilderness

at the bricks' edge. Hands sunk deep
in lemon balm, heather and yarrow, she named

each herb she touched, the paths in her palms
like vines in her flesh, weaving and unweaving

an uncertain redemption. He was haunted
by jasmine, the memory of jasmine in forests

long empty, ghostly petals gathered and swept
by wind, by city traffic along pavement, and

descending into the walled underground, speeding
with the speeding light of the subway's thrust

against oblivion, and from the edge of thought
he cried out to her *throw earth on me,*

you can, and from the garden tiles she rose,
lifted her soiled fingers until the blank

in his chest and the blank before him
began to fill with leaves.

The Rothko Chapel, Houston, Early Spring

I sit in a room of black paintings, listening to the walls of day open into darkness,
when a shaft of light at the ceiling's center moves into one canvas, creates an opening
purple, rose, and what I hear instead of silence is a line, a poet's voice,

God sent me to the sea for pearls.

If I could, I would follow the call glowing in the painting's lower corner,
enter the gray-black surface and sail the turbulence which is every hero's sea.

A boy I loved believed he could enter a rock with his thumbnail. He would trace
the invisible crack in the stone's surface his grandfather had polished
that he might sail the darkness, find whatever he could in a rock formed by fire.

I sit in a room of black paintings, chapel walls silent as stones, and as inanimate, until

God sent me to the sea for pearls

becomes the storyline breaking out of time at the water's edge,
looking from the porch of the sea onto the sea's dark expanse, and diving
into that rhythmic infinite for the stone one must pull from the clay bottom, gray matter,
the luminous rock within the stone of the oyster, the skull.
The sea-stone is a pearl.

But I meant to sing about the boy I loved who dreamed in his madness he had
swallowed a pearl—
a god making the stories of men, a man making the stories of gods,
a boy building song out of story. I sit in a room of paintings no longer black, listening,
and what I hear instead of silence is a line, a voice, the boy speaking:

Every dream is ancient: A boy lives by the River Min
in the province of Sichuan, gathers grasses for his living,
and when one day he pulls from the soil
a pearl tinged with rose,
he buries it in his mother's rice jar.

Grass, rice, coins in abundance make a village covetous,
and when they come to seize the boy's treasure,
he swallows the jewel, his belly burns with thirst
until he drinks the river dry,
and his back swells with scales and wings,
the sky with rain, a mother's heart with tears.

This is the story of the dragon's pearl, of a culture's call for creation,
and what belongs to a people belongs to the one man. The myth of a pearl becomes
the story of a boy who wanted to die, to let the river enter him until he was cold as stone,
until the stone of madness he imagined lodged in his skull could shine,

illuminate a world.
These are the paintings of a man who wanted to die, to penetrate stone until he
could not see,
a blind man wanting a second chance, second sight.

God sent them to the sea for pearls.

These are the paintings of a man who wanted to live,
to return from stone in a burst of light, rose-tinged, a pearl, a coin, a luminous other.

This is the struggle between story and song.
The pearl is the rock animated, the clay bottom resurrected and ascending.

God sends us to the sea for pearls,
for luminous stone, animated by the call of creation.

The boy I loved wanted to die listening to the sea. He believed, in death, he could
penetrate stone,
enter the rock-hard earth with his thumbnail, rose-colored half-mooned cuticle of stone
digging into darkness, into the blood-black river of his wrist.

The boy I loved wanted to live, a pearl, a coin, a luminous other life he would invent, ancient life, beckoned by an ancient call. He believed he must die to begin again.

I sit in a room of paintings purple and black and rose, listening to light, the voices of the dead swelling like a sea in the back of my skull, and I look at my hands, ask them for a spell, a god's incantatory call to dust.

In memory of Ian Davidson
(1962–2012)

Self-Portrait: Trieste

I am listening for what is not there,
the tonality of silence, the blank space
between the spoken lines of a conversation,
what lives in the eyes, the lilt of a head.
I know nothing more
of history, American soldiers than the smell
of one man's green uniform,
the cold metallic stars on his chest.
I accumulate the absences, study them,
as if they were the rhinestone buttons
on my mother's best suit, shining like stars,
but not stars. I will learn to live
by the boundaries language makes,
a child tottering at the edge
of speech and an old mattress
in a Trieste hotel room at the border
of Italy, Yugoslavia, Slovenia—
forty, fifty years of naming, renaming.

Sorites and Sand

Mrs. Schmetterling has been thinking about boundaries,
how the borders of countries and of gardens overlap,
how words themselves melt into one another—prefix, suffix, root—
until she is now swept away
in a sea of sentence upon sentence, drowning.
Recently she learned she has confused the words
sostre and *sorites*, *sisters* and *a heap of sand*.
What words she wonders are necessary for sister
syllogisms to build upon each other,
not by heaping but weaving,
like the loom work of a great queen.
Mrs. Schmetterling could build a kingdom
on the threads of a shroud. She could stretch strands
of cowhide wide to build a city.
She could be a woman poised to speak
if these thoughts running wild in her head
could converge, compose the seamless fabric
of a slow-moving river, each syllable,
a rivulet, a warp or weft thread
floated inextricably into each sister stitch,
world to word, word to world.

Loom

It was not a question of deceit but of survival
that she sat long nights in moonlight at the loom,
and what she wove by day in verdant colors, by night,
with blue-streaked eyes, she would unravel,
stitching in the half-illumined dark
another fabric, each shuttle's stroke, a stirring
like a wingbeat in the surface of
a shawl almost translucent, a second skin.

All she knew moved through her skin
until, tongueless, she sang the colors of fire,
her threads, the words of a room
among rooms in the larger dwelling,
until out of the golden fabric of her shroud,
a woman rose up.

The Palace at 4:00 a.m.

"Memory's nakedness is like a bone that will not decay."
—Liu Xiaobo

Alberto Giacometti understood the house of childhood
to be a house of bones, or more accurately

in this case, of bare wood, glass, wire—
the sculpture's naked frame, a skeleton of mother memory.

What I remember as a child is a dream in which I walk
along the steel girders of an anonymous building,

a labyrinth of metal rising into the night sky's
pitch black, the narrow beams like blocks of ice or fire

beneath my feet, each step a tightrope dance above an abyss.
Unlike the *Palace* no objects hang seductively.

No Surrealist's invitation into sleep. I wander endlessly
from beam to beam, imprisoned in an emptiness

whose only gift is silence.
Mother was an absence. The invisible

walls of a house. An empty amphitheater strung with
rhinestones shining like stars.

Mother. An elusive sparkling.
Giacometti divides the *Palace* with a pane of glass,

a transparent skin, a membrane, what we see but cannot touch,
what cannot touch us, a brittle veil between lives.

If I could speak to the girl suspended, balancing,
holding her breath, I would tell her how she will outlive

the inner dark, how the glass pane will shatter
into cerulean fragments, how she will come to wear

these shards like buttons sewn on a woman's suit coat.
Each tiny stone, a star or bone, fastened against her chest

by frayed thread whispering *open, open*,
to each rib, vertebra, as a voice in a dream might

choreograph the tenuous constellation of hours,
burning coals, lemon balm, a flowering.

II

In the Heart's Cellar, Sleepless

The Angel of Architecture

You are the one I call in my sleep,
mother of absences, the one whose doorways
grow wide, open onto side yards, gardens
where ferns and the thorny vines of bougainvillea
trail among rocks and the terra cotta tiles.
Your body is a trellis for climbing
jasmine and the orphaned world.
You wear stucco and smooth-cut stone.
Your moss-stained dress offers walls
to those whose beds sit among ashes,
under bridges, float on slow-moving rivers.
You appear on downtown streets
in the largest of cities, in dung heaps,
old appliance stores, abandoned warehouses.
You hover above the fire sale, the hands
of women peddling losses, and weave
with fingers which stream like hair,
like rivulets of iron-sweet milk
from your breasts, the house of childhood,
the heart's medieval architecture.

Mrs. Schmetterling Thinks of Her Heart

Mrs. Schmetterling thinks of herself as a visible whole
not as parts, a conglomeration of molecules.
She is not a scientific woman.
When she thinks of heart, that rocking, flopping in her chest,
she does not see in her mind's eye a muscle
or chambers, or bloody arteries twitching, rather
she sees cranes rising from a marsh *en masse*,
their extended wings a white blanket of fluttering
that propel her to her feet and then to the mailbox.
She loves letters, or the thought of letters,
and the oceans they have crossed, braiding the world
together like a handful of hair resting along her shoulder.
She is enviable in this way, for she makes all things
rise up from within. Even the most disparate of objects or ideas—
the reading of Wittgenstein's *Tractatus* and schnitzel recipes,
the map pencil drawings of her childhood
and the hubris of war's vowels, Lwów, Lvov, L'viv—
seem to coalesce within her own warm body,
her own inner life and the world's.

Religion by Design

From an exhibit of student photographs

Those nights when I do sleep deeply,
I dream of rust, broken angels, gargoyles,
their tongues exposed, teeth bared,
two stone swans, necks become serpents,
eyes, the eye of a dragon,
a keyhole, doorbell, an entrance.

In the vestibule of an old church is a clock,
stopped, 11:35, day or night? Then stained glass
windows distorting the light into dogma.
An infant angel squats, heaves stone
over his shoulder in a garden
built of cathedral courtyard and sky,

torn sky where a broken Christ sobs, presides.
Outside the frame a single angel sits.
Both cherubic and gaunt, she is misplaced,
the career she imagines, ruptured.
She is not prepared for air, each breath
an accomplishment. She lives at a horizon,

a creature between worlds. She may stand,
open her wings to the white walls, empty air
swallowing stars, or she may seek re-entry:
shattered glass, known colors and halftones
dissolving into gradations of gray. If I could,
I would dream her a mortal body, muscled, singing.

Women Harvesting: Virgins, Widows, Wives

After a triptych by Konrad von Hirsau, ca. 1200

It might be von Hirsau believed he composed
a celebration, these wood panels brushed
with egg and tempera, a medieval man's rendering
of the rich work of women in his world,
or he might be any century's man
harnessing the unruly longing beauty stirs
within him. Either way, he names them
after himself like daughters. . .

virgins, these young women not yet touched,
their bodies bundled like the sheaves
they carry, unbind only for each other.
Content with what they do not know,
their bodies are the swinging of the scythe,
they are the gathering
folds of their robes, they are the bending,
swaying of torsos, knees
yielding. Why need they resist,
these passing beauties whose arms
harvest slowly, one sheaf at a time?

And these women, widows, what are they
but resistance? They bend beneath
the scythe's weight, heave
a full season on their breasts,
keep, for companions, sisters and ghosts and stones.
They wear white. . .shrouds, larval veils.

They weep for their lost men, bereft
of shoulders, arms, those bearded faces.
Is this grief, to work alone, a woman among women,
the garden become a field, the field a landscape
of stone, or is this plenitude?
Do they smell of absence
or of the grain they harvest?

And I, wife and witness, turn to you
in the third panel, one man among wives. . .
Do you know the woman who works at your side,
the curve of her neck, the small shoulders,
or have you mistaken
the urgency of her voice, her body

for strength, good faith?
She stoops below a radiant tree,
bends and bends until her wrists can touch
her red shoes. No. From her back
a small tree grows white,
the possibility of radiance,
like the box of seeds she carries

at her right side. Surely you see this tree,
this abstract of a tree, the shadow
of what burns inside her. Open your hand,
lay your palm against her throat, release
the brown dress she wears like sheaves loosened,
falling, until the body's work dissolves,
a field on fire, a fiery harvest.

Mrs. Schmetterling Considers the Beautiful

Mrs. Schmetterling looks on beauty
as an interior landscape, the moonrise of her imagination.
When she closes her eyes, she sees the room's ceiling
fill first with billowing shadows, then a pinpoint of
light that blooms into a blue-black shining, then
the brilliant blue of coronal plasma that could
be the widening eye of God. Or a host of
angels navigating a great abyss, their
wings clapping out light. But Mrs. Schmetterling is
skeptical of the sublime. She does not trust a transcendence
that will come to her on the day the world ends.
She believes in what she can see, hold
in her mind's eye. Cold, hard snow
in muddy clumps melting, kicked aside.
Chestnut trees lining the avenues, their tiny candelabras
of blossom upon blossom, at the bud's edge, waiting.
Ubiquitous sparrows flitting among the branches,
then among tulips when they bloom at last.
The romantic vestige of old musicians
spilling their song into the square.
The other music of boot clicks
on stone. All this she carries
as the roiling blue that rises
like a wall, a tidal wave
of light behind her eyes.

Portrait of the Artist's Wife with Pegasus

Józef Mehoffer, oil on canvas, 1914

Behind her, the whole of Art Nouveau frolics—
a white and red beribboned Pegasus
prances in a night sky,
bare-breasted mermaids stream hair
and scaled tails,
bob in a William Morris wallpaper sea
and swoon skyward
into the chest of the horse—

while she sits dressed in black
from the wide-brimmed ruffled hat, feather boa,
to the leather gloves laid flat
on the chintz skirt
smoothed carefully over her knees.
Even her wrists are covered,
one inch of ornamental lace fanning
out from the sleeve.

All of this the artist observes with precision,
but what she sees
is her husband's face
tethered to the canvas as if by invisible thread,
and she has dressed in black
because she mourns
the direction of the light
in his eyes.

Kosovo, April Mornings

A man moves a woman in a wheelbarrow under a gray sky.
They look directly into the camera.
In a boxcar a weeping man holds a child sucking a biscuit.
Six women in faded dresses and scarves surround a small boy,
mourn. Two arms reach from a train window
for bread held out to them by anonymous hands. *Ethnic Albanians.*

I could stay with these newspaper photographs at the kitchen table
over coffee, travel the road to Pristina, Macedonia, Monte Negro
in my mind, but this is not my suffering, my life—
Make me a stone—the heart of a stone—I turn away,
think of my own day—classes I must teach, the four late library books
stacked by the door, my daughter's voice lesson, another softball game,
branches fallen from the ash tree and sprawling on the lawn,
the tree trimmers we can't afford—I fold the newspaper,
throw it with others into a green plastic bin, to set by the street.
Tomorrow's Tuesday, recycling.

Another morning. The pictures pile up, like postcards,
here at my kitchen table in my American house where I imagine I am safe,
and exile is a newspaper photograph. I lock the front door,
leave for school, downtown. Or exile is a sign above the Main Street
Fire Sale—*New losses arrive daily*. I think of my son in a different city,
his voice wails out a Robert Johnson song on the tape I'm playing.
I see my mother's face at sixteen in the hand-tinted photograph
hung in the hallway—*He has her mouth,* my brother-in-law says of my son.
Beautiful mouths. A woman's, a man's. Beautiful, vanishing mouths.
But the song persists. I turn up the tape, keep driving.

Refugees. If I could meet their eyes over miles of earth, ocean—
if newsprint were a kind of porous soul, a membrane of transport.
See the face of the woman in faded red, kneeling at the waist of the boy—
she has my friend's face, she could be Audrey, I could know this woman.
See the woman lying on a makeshift hospital bed in a Macedonian camp,
reaching for her infant swaddled in blue muslin—it could be 1953,
I know this child born at the Yugoslav border, recognize my mother's hair.

I can wish to be a stone, in the heart of a stone,
or I can write this down, paragraph, postcard, poem,
abbreviated record of a moment in a life, lives—
two particular lives held against the anonymity of our vanishing.
See the green of her skirt tucked into the wheelbarrow,
the patchwork quilt covering her, her white scarf, his long khaki coat.

A man and a woman move between worlds—what they've left,
where they're headed. They may have had a kitchen table,
a garden beneath the window, books, a child, a house—human face of a house
inscribing the landscape of stone, turning fallen trees to architecture.
I can inscribe the dirt where he walks, where the one wheel
of the cart in which she rides drags, tracks their presence,
their real human presence, its passage.

In an Amsterdam Hotel

In an Amsterdam hotel we push twin beds together
so that I can lie lengthwise against your back.

We have been here five days, and each morning
I wake to a black and white photograph,

the kind you see in any decent hotel room
where buildings, trees, shrubs stand at a shoreline,

and are mirrored in the water below.
Twin landscapes each growing out of the other,

an irony of rootedness that rises, falls,
then manages this meeting at margin of lake and sky.

It is an ordinary scene, typical I think,
of the photographer's fascination with doubleness,

a halving of the world into positive and negative,
what we are, defined by what we are not,

what we love, by what we must let go.
On these mattresses, our bodies are a landscape of rootedness.

In only a few hours we will rise, dress,
meet separate planes headed for separate continents,

and test the hypothesis of landscape photographers
on separate shorelines.

My Husband's Face

I wander the creekbeds of your forehead
leisurely, lightly, a Chopin nocturne
moving beneath my feet. I wander the dream
rolling beneath the creekbeds,
of a man in love with the things of the world,
a black ash tree or rounded stones or
the woman who wanders a sleeping face.

Barefoot in a cotton dress, I wade,
skip stones in the dark pools beneath your eyes,
the late sun smoothing my cheek like a hand,
your hand opening into undulating hair,
an ocean, a dark continent, the night sky of youth,
in the dream we share,
in the landscape of your face.

Under the Moon

A painting by Billy Hassell

A man takes the long way home,
sees in the blue-black dark the figure of a wolf,
    the shape of darkness
swallowing up all where he walks.
        The wolf contains constellations
    and the man moves under the stars

    in the wolf's belly, swims among them, lost,
afraid of the shape darkness takes.
    He begins again.
        A man walks home under the moon as if
the sky were a blank canvas, a page of a sketchbook
    he keeps in his back pocket, a map

    of tangled branches where a raven perches,
fire under her wing. He holds the moon
    in his palm like fireflies he's trapped,
until his knuckles shine,
        and with that light he paints
    the moon, the blue-black night,

    the raven, the fish, the luminous wolf.
He reaches into the canvas,
    turns his hands to the raven's nest,
        rolls the night-eggs in his palm,
until they are hard as the moon or lapis lazuli,
    stones which open,

each crystalline face a door.
The man enters, is immersed in blue stone, in darkness
        among constellations he can never contain,
among angels, raven-like, haunting.
                Or, the dark inhabits him
        and he devours grief until it sparkles,

        rises like angels or stars, like fireflies
released into a night meadow, soaring,
        leaving his body.
                A man takes the long way home,
and what he finds under the moon
        is the loose weave of hand and eye,

        pigment and light, an interior
tide tethering him to the night-
        violet grass, releasing him
                from his own, small reflection.

April Storm

I lie on a bare mattress watching
blades of the ceiling fan slice lightning,
bat it in pieces from wall to wall,
fireworks in the room's night sky.

I am thinking of you, and Habermas,
and of the logic of lightning,
how reasonably nature behaves
catapulted from sky to earth

to the rooms of human sleep,
and how unreasonable I am—heart-lens
awake in the dark, filtering nature's design—
to feel in the pulse of rain pelting the window

your fingers of weeks, months ago,
still tangled in my hair.

Passage

"Blessed is the soul where time does not run." Michelangelo

I.
If I could write from the soul where time does not run.
If I could open a door in stone.
At the cherrywood desk where I work, I watch our black ash tree
spread six separate limbs, each a trunk, a decade in the life of a house
opening, splitting with age and the song of owls.
I count the branches, trace each departure like a line
among lines in the web of a human palm upturned.

An urban forester tells me this tree will fall sooner than I want to believe.
Every tree compartmentalizes its injuries, he says.
I say, *Seal off your wounds beautiful aging ash, believe
in your own healing, seal out the too sure voice of youth.*
Angular, knotted, an old woman's arms outstretched, arthritic,
these dark trunks, streaked with cracks in bark and dried pulp, become
a tree opening.

II.
If I could reach into rock.
If I could carve out an opening for voices trapped
in the weight, the rapture of the body.
I would swim into stone, a river,
the way one man forms another man's face

out of silence, uncut marble, and names the sublime
body of a man, whispers *David, David* into each ear,
penetrating stone with his voice, reaching into his chest

like a god, building cornice and doorframe, one rib at a time,
safe passage for the human heart.

III.
The faces of the Pieta weep stone tears until
rock-hard salt water flows at their feet, along the Basilica floor,
beyond vestibule and cathedral doors, and descends one hundred stairs
into the Florentine streets.
The tree we have loved sings with rain in a dry season,
opens skyward.

IV.
It is August, and the sage below the ash tree stands
still and gray and does not bloom.
Its lilac blossoms must first be imagined. I close my eyes.
It is July 27, 1999. My mother's mother, Edna Iola Edwards, is dead.
The sage blooms three days and stops, desert flower, desert time.

This summer I wait, for lilacs, for death,
for a second chance to stand beside my grandmother's open casket
and lay my pearl earrings beneath her hands, small stones
wrapped in a vanishing body, as she once laid
her own earrings in mine in the backseat of an old Cadillac
because I asked her for something of hers to keep, small stones
laid into my slowly vanishing hands. I was afraid
to bury even the smallest part of myself with her.

V.

To enter the earth, to find a door in.

A passageway, an exchange, one woman's gift to another

in departure. I whisper my grandmother's name, *Edna, Edna.*

I listen for her voice calling my name,

wait for her palm on my forehead.

VI.

I have my own children now, one son, one daughter

and with each coming and going,

I move to an interior tide, as if I contained oceans,

watched the smallness of the human project in those waters.

To find a door in is to build a door out.

When I open my eyes, the ink I write with

is perfumed with sage, and my own children are not yet home.

They live in a world of streets and theaters, cars and shopping malls.

A doorway lives between worlds, an invitation.

I watch for them in the darkness.

VII.

If I could light their passage out of night.

If I could reach into the western sky, hold Venus in my hands.

(Starlight is a stone opening.)

I close the window shade, step away from the cherrywood desk,

to unlock the door of a house we still share

(Light beneath the rock's skin pulses like a voice. Michelangelo heard this light

in the ecstatic moment of flesh on stone.)

where the black ash tree stands tenuous, sheltering,
(He opened his hands to listen. Time stopped.)
and I lie down beside my sleeping husband,
his arms, the rhythm of his breath, my pillow.

For Tony, and for the Morning

For centuries, the river Saraswati has washed
the small villages of Rajasthan with loveliness.

I am told that the villagers are craftsmen
of a cloth that, when bathed in the sands and
waters of the river, is cast in rose.
They then carve small motifs in wood where
the block is inked with the pale blood of vegetables
and the cloth spread for printing.

Just last evening, I was held in loveliness
by Sanganeri cloth, your gift to me,
and I noticed in the wearing a single thread
like spun light which appeared, reappeared between
each tiny earthen blossom and the dye's bleeding.
Now as I wake, I imagine that

you have come to me over centuries,
in a thread of light, to wash me rose.

Braiding

For Chelsea

I'm braiding my daughter's hair,
crossing over one strand and one strand.
Leaf-shadows play on the closed blind,
rippling, rippling.
Nothing keeps in the continuum
of light and wind outside the window.
I hold wildness in my hand.
We continue, one strand and one strand,
the undulating curls and coils
falling along her neck, her shoulders.
I drop one hair, then another.
Though I'm not much good at this,
she is patient. Her head in my hands,
she leans in, tugs away, as do I,
crafting what we can of the morning.
I'd like to believe I've saved her
from chaos, but more likely,
she humors me, and before afternoon
she'll shake her braids,
let all that hair unravel.

Story Child

It is afternoon, late April,
        and the building's ceiling is like a greenhouse
    or a temple, the light from vaulted, triangular windows
filtered and falling across your right cheek, your shoulder
    as you stand before me—priest, wizard, shaman—
        speaking until your voice cracks, and I can see my father

    the afternoon he left me on the steps
        of an old Austin dormitory, his arms outstretched
    as if I were a bride, my father's hand on mine, shifting my love
from one man to another among rows of lawn chairs
    and a makeshift altar, or I could be the boy in the poem

    whose father turns him upside down, shakes him
        until the small piece of flesh which strangles him
    is set free and he vomits his death back onto itself,
gives birth to a ring of gray smoke, his own ghost rising up
    where the new boy is forming. In Alaskan seafaring tribes,
        a pregnant woman wears in her hair a wooden comb

    carved with a tiny inverted man born out of a frog's mouth.
        She believes the frog guards her child's passage
    through water into air and light, just as I wore
the carved ivory idol of Ashanti women—its swollen head, straight body—
    like a cross. But birth is not magic,
        for the infant cut from me that late May morning lived

    because he had a second chance—a boy well-formed but trapped
        in a body that would not open. We were lucky.
    My closest neighbor has no children,

but her whole yard's a garden where fern and honeysuckle,
        iris and asters thrive. I see her the afternoon she opens
                a carton of red-winged ladybugs she's ordered, sets them free

      among plants and trees, as protection, then turns,
             picks a lavender garlic blossom, sings to my daughter
        who spins herself round and round in Susan's grass,
Ladybug, Ladybug, fly away home. Your house is on fire.
      Your children are gone. I think of how the African folktales
        of Ekoi explain their genesis, how Mouse goes everywhere,

      watching the heart's secret doings, weaving from each a story child
           in a different colored gown, white, red, blue, black.
        The stories became her children and lived in her house
and served her because she had no children of her own. The morning
      I read aloud this prologue, begin with my students the tale
      of how the spider obtained the Sky-god's stories,

      I find Aminah at her desk writing, *My imaginary twin has no voice.*
          She hums and when she hums the children come to listen,
        the flowers bloom and blossom until one day she slips,
cracks her head so that sand, songs, flowers, spill forth
      and all the ground except where she lies catches fire.
      Now, because in this moment of vaulted light

      I believe you love me, the room enlarges, shines,
          and the story children come spilling like sand or songs
        from my skull, my mouth, tumbling free along my thighs,
my parted knees, like the brown gossamer husk the she-spider spins,
      torn open into a cloud of children, until she can step
        beside and over each one, leaving them, letting them go.

III

If Grief Were a Bird

Serinette

After Eavan Boland

I live in a mortgaged house on a city street
where I wake to traffic not birdsong.
In the loose weave of ligustrum beyond the window
a single robin sits, flies at the glass,
moves from the outside in, but cannot enter.
My mother named me Robin, moved her hands

along my throat that ached when I could not sleep,
when the wound was a voice moving inside me.
She painted birds which twittered, sparrows,
finches, a pair of *hooded nuns,* their tiny heads
black or brown velvet, luminous surfaces,
silent, still, her two good children.

This morning among twenty-four windows,
in a house made of glass, I think of you whom I love,
man watching from another window, a different room.
You are the *satinwood box on gilded feet*
in the living room's farthest corner, the *blond body*
inscribed with songbirds, branches, the serinette

which teaches me to sing, a middle-aged woman
becoming her mother, and the reluctant bird stammers,
groans a little in my chest. How can I sing when I know
I will die? The robin in the garden pushes hard
against the pane, has no patience, insists.
When I know I will die, how can I keep silent?

I open the window sealed with years of paint
shutting out sound. I let the bird in, that will panic
at what it finds, closed corners of a room confining flight,
turning song to traffic. I let the bird in,
that will be changed by the room which is not sky,
and I, in a room changed by flight, I listen.

On Rereading "Home Burial"

In Frost's poem the woman misunderstands,
     takes the man's motion for something less
          than grief, each plunge of the spade

at the dead child's grave, a violation.
     She does not know how much he loves her,
          how with this digging, emptying,

filling, smoothing, he polishes each face on the jewel
     of her grief as if it were a new cut stone
          bearing a name she refuses to speak.

Words are stones their voices hurl, break
     against each other till each becomes gravel
          covering a child's mound, a marriage.

This morning we stand in the back grass watching a young jay
     try its wings, parents flying wildly about the fence.
          We laugh, hear ourselves in each strained call

the old birds make to the child leaving.
     We lean together, our bodies become the garden,
          stalks of purple fountain grass, salvia bent

beneath the weight of blossoming. We return to coffee,
     books, the ease of Sunday, when I hear it:
          a mother's shrill lament, wild panic.

You're first to see the dead jay at the bottom
     of the back porch steps, body mutilated,
          predator vanished. I turn away as you scoop

into your palm what's left of feathers just coloring.
        You move to the plum tree at the garden's edge,
            lift my trowel, the handle shaky, rotting,

and thrust it deep into the black loam
        at the sapling's base. This could be one of ours,
            and I see you dig for each of us,

parents of sky and earth, that birds might shriek
        about your head, blaming, blaming,
            as I would, were this my lost child,

while you go on digging the dead jay's grave—
        digging, emptying, filling, smoothing.
            You would do this for me.

Notes for a Larger Poem

I am on a train or in a room moving
        slowly, rhythmically into sunrise.
                The windows, jewel-like,

refract the landscape into fragments
        barely visible, blurred, vanishing.
                I turn away.

In the room's corner is a cardboard box
        holding all that is left
                of my father.

Shreds of his best suit and a green blanket.
        The smell of starch, tweed, old shaving lotion,
                the body of memory, rotting. . .

I kneel, cradle the box like a child
        or would, if my arms could reach,
                but the enormity of space

opening before me becomes a blankness
        so large, I cannot yet imagine it
                a possibility for more

than dissolution.

Viaticum

When you love the one you bury, you plan the journey.
My sister and I buried our father with supplies.
His viaticum, his cell phone and a small blue bird,
wings extended in flight, carved from a Polish linden.

In the blue-black tunnel behind my eyes
where the small lightning of sleep sparkles,
there is a linden.

The linden is often an ornamental tree and gives birth
to the lime blossom, pungent, nectar-producing, *some say* healing.
Linden wood is soft, easily worked, ideal for crafting
wind instruments, electric guitar bodies, window blinds.

In the blue-black tunnel where the dead lie
and the small lightning of long sleep sparkles,
there is a voice.

My father hummed. He always carried a tune in his head.
My son plays electric guitar, and his voice is old
like Blind Lemon Jefferson or Lightnin' Hopkins.
He carries a shrill breath behind his tongue that rises.

From the blue-black tunnel behind my eyes
birdsong rises and the small lightning of morning
sparkles the living awake.

The day my father died, he used his new cell phone
to call me home. I saved that voice for months until one day
it disappeared among messages set to expire, leaving
in my palm tangled paths of an uncertain ascent.

Spoken to the Evening

After Ingeborg Bachmann

At the raised blind's edge beyond this office window,
the pocked disc of the moon rises white in a violet sky,
like a Communion wafer dipped in wine and fire.

I have worked too long in a white room
where no songs visit me,
and transcendence sleeps twelve hours a day.

O moon, well of white heat in an infinite sky,
if I shouted into you, would I hear my own voice
echoed back against the glass, or would something greater speak?

If I tossed into you the two faded coins I rub
between thumb and forefinger, against this suit pocket's silk lining,
would you swallow my wish,

or would these pennies turn to transport?
Over the highway rising above the downtown warehouse district,
over the city jail's manicured brick

and the abandoned pump station's moss-covered brick,
the moon moves out of reach, higher, smaller, like a child's god
and the evening reddens into darkness.

August Garden

In the August garden in moonlight
the iron bells rust, the wind itself is rust
and silence. What's left of water in the birdbath
becomes the stone which holds it.
The frog, the lilies, all pale green stone.
Green veins on white caladiums
narrow toward stems drooping,
leaning toward the clay.

If I were a child, I would read or kneel,
wait out emptiness till I could feel a rising
in my chest like laughter or blood or song,

but here on the stone steps, I ride
the rhythm of loss. It loosens my hair
at the roots, robs it of color strand by strand.
It pulses blue in the raised veins
in my hands, breasts, in the spreading
veins behind my knees, dirtied blue
marble visible only when I stop,
turn to look back.

A wise man loves water. I long to believe
contentment moves like a river within us,
exceeding time and desire.

August caladiums shine like white stones,
heart-shaped, blank but for vascular
traces of green. I long to believe
these are the traces of rapture

not yet forgotten, bits of green
nourishing the form they inscribe,
sustaining them just above the soil
so that it appears they wait a while,
live as long as they can.

In the Balance of Final Things

Mrs. Schmetterling has been reading *The Egyptian Book*
of the Dead and now when she lies down to sleep
she sees in her mind's eye the balance of final things.
She imagines herself before a tribunal of gods
in human masks. She counts each face like sheep—
old Marx, old Miłosz, one, two. The young Baczyński, three.
Joseph Stalin in a white moustache, baby Adolf in a white smock,
the Black Madonna of Częstochowa, four, five, six.
She sees Europe, east and west, under a sky of fireworks and ash.
She keeps counting, watches the high scales
suspended above her head, one pan drooping
beneath the weight of a single stone.
Mrs. Schmetterling considers her life, waits for the moment
she must place her own heart in the balance.
She wonders what punishment waits for a heart too light.
She regrets laughter, the warmth of her down comforter,
her own fate lucky, random, unearned.

Oświęcim

I.

I walk through the detritus of history,
a tourist. Our guide is Polish. She knows
each crematorium chimney,
each pond of human ash
will become
a gallery of faces floating
upside down in a smoked glass floor.

We enter the room slowly, almost on tiptoe,
watch whole families recede and rise.
We could fall
into this black glass like water,
rise bleeding, bloated
with tears.

II.

A glass case stretching the full length of a corridor wall
holds sixty years
of braids and strands and mattes
stacked, kilos of a terrible beauty.

Strands of hair move beneath my skin,
a vascular braiding
of heart and lungs and limbs,
blue veins, blue hair
knotted, writhing.
I wake alone,
in a tangle of starched sheets,
unable to cry out or swallow.

III.
The cedars are crowded with ghosts
who wind in and out of the tall trunks,
carrying suitcases,
straightening their caps,
loosening their blouses or vests in the heat.

They are waiting for something.
I can see them.
This is no photograph.

IV.
The streets of Oświęcim are crowded with children.
It is afternoon. School must be out
for they wait at bus stops,
buy ice cream,
crush clods of dried mud with their boot heels.
As far as we can see
the cherries and acacias bloom
white as ice cream, cotton candy,
cumulus clouds rising above a death camp.

Borowski's Suicide

July 1, 1951,
six days after the birth of his daughter, Małgorzata

What did he see in that infant face,
ghost of memory, fresh from the belly's gauze,

his palm laid against the tiny skull,
each blue vein in the temple pulsing?

Wrenched from the gauze of memory,
the train car floor littered with children.

Faces flung down, the belly's ghosts.
The floors cleared for the rapes to come,

a young woman, a sheer cotton dress,
the belly's gauze, torn and torn.

Tadeusz Borowski, Polish Catholic,
member of the *Kanada* crew, Auschwitz

survivor, communist, journalist, poet.
A man walking among the living dead

woke one morning to his daughter's face,
wrenched from the belly's gauze,

gauze of memory, living ghost swaddled
in the dreamlike pulse of his step.

No stable. No star. No
breath of Elijah at the door.

In Kazimierz

Walking with head bowed,
the shadow of a butterfly on ground ivy,
the soul's movement through this middle earth.

What Mrs. Schmetterling Wants

Mrs. Schmetterling wants nothing more
than the landscape, the city's opening
onto streets of stones, shops, small wrought-iron tables
hung with umbrellas, set with cloth napkins, beer.
She meanders among high-rise apartment buildings, window boxes
bursting with petunias, cloud whites, bubble gum pinks,
the purples of bruises, buried blood.
She watches the train station walls blooming with graffiti.
Mrs. Schmetterling does not want history.
She wants the graffiti to color old concrete, cover the blood.
She lives between kitsch and the weight of stones,
the exhibit of painted noses and torsos and giant sunflowers
at the city gate, and the gate itself.
She wants nothing more than her soul's wilderness
taking hold at the city's edge, spreading like milkweed
in the garden plot that no one owns,
no one owns.

Revisions

A man searches for God.
He searches the dark cavities of libraries,
drinks each book like water out of rock,
ingests the thin white pages,
a manna he holds in his mouth until it sings.
He searches fire escapes, paintings, subways.
He searches restaurants, Roman temples,
his own ruins. When he dreams,
he seeks a heavenly father
to replace the earthly one, long vanished,
and when he wakes, he searches the still sacred
body of his wife for a god, for a father,
for a son. When a son comes,
he glimpses the beginning of divinity,
calls him angel, and tells the boy a story
of the milk-white steed made of lightning
an angel harnessed
to carry a great prophet into heaven.

A man searches for God.
He searches biblical texts, histories, the ambitions
of philosophers. He walks on his hands,
turns the world upside down. He runs and runs.
He searches the constant humming in his head,
searches his Welsh father's poems
for the tune he carries in his chest,
within the sea-green sky of a coat
where metallic stars float, form tiny constellations.
He seeks a heavenly father
to replace the earthly one, long dead,

searches the sacred body of his wife for a god,
for a father, for a son, but no son comes.
The man has a daughter, a Thumbelina of divinity.
Each day he reads to her, she listens
until all the gods of the world
live in her eyes, and there he sees
his own small reflection.

A woman searches for God.
She searches temples and books, altar cloths and gardens.
She searches the center of peonies,
the face of each man she has loved.
She searches her husband's chest, each shoulder,
the smooth, dark skin beneath his eyes.
The woman has a son and in this child's face
she glimpses the beginning of divinity:
God in diapers, God in a baseball cap,
God with a Fender Stratocaster strapped to his chest.
What he creates with his breath, his hands
is reenactment, a legacy of absence.
His song is the grief of a woman who is no son,
the grief of a daughter who is no father
for the god who made her. His is the song
of all fatherless sons, and he sings that suffering
until it becomes an ecstasy, and he lifts
that ecstasy heavenward like a prayer.

A woman searches for God.
She searches kitchens, poems, the wilderness
of heather growing up at her feet.

She watches the sky, looks for the constellation
of sisters, of a vessel opening, spilling water.
She searches yarrow stalks, the broken lines
of trigrams, tarot cards.
She searches her own full breasts,
the wreath of eucalyptus and sweet basil
she hangs above a child's cradle.
The woman has a daughter, and in this child
grows a different dream of divinity:
God in lace, God in a leotard,
God with a girl's face, kneeling beneath a tree.
Beside the black ash tree, fallen, in starlight,
the boy this girl holds plants a garden in her mouth,
and in her throat bloom stars and wounds
and Goethe's *Roslein, Roslein, Roslein*.
What she tastes is the grief of a woman orphaned
for the garden she takes into her mouth,
a woman guilty for a man's solitude,
for a god's grief at his children leaving,
and she sings that lament
until it becomes a possibility,
giedd, giedd, giedd, whispering forgiveness,
forgiveness, and a woman's original splendor.

How to Paint Light

To paint light you must return to that first raw surface
like the wall of a room

in the lives of rooms you never knew.
Return to sheetrock, shiplap, memoryless stone,

or to striations of sun at the bottom of a lake
before shadow accumulates layer by layer.

You must work backwards against pigment,
and dust. Pain and ash. The swift current

of human memory sealing out dawn.
You must close your eyes until you see

your dozing grandmother rock history to sleep.
You are a child in her arms.

Winter Litany

Kraków, March, 2004

I stand on *Wawel Hill*
in early March and morning snow
falls in flocks
tiny paper cranes
descending blowing dissolving
one into another
on the cobblestone walk
an avalanche of light

I believe this must be
what death is

this alternate
shining and melting, shining and flying

Cubist Self-Portrait
Where Each Surface Is Time

I.
You begin as a small stain
in the hollow of hollows
on the wall of mother gut
where myth and blood meet,
blend, bruise.
This is your first sin.

You dare to grow.
Like linden limbs, soft, pliant,
good for carving small birds, flutes,
you stretch out your bones,
a far reaching thought, a humming.
Each love becomes reenactment,
your life's unfolding, a tattoo
of concentric stains.

And then your father dies.
The myth of your life becomes
a dead rabbit in a magician's top hat.
A silence of hours. A horizon
opening before you:
White sunset.
Blank movie screen.
And you watch, waiting
for something to happen,
but nothing does.

II.
A woman kneels in a garden, breaks open
each amaryllis pod in her palm, peels back
the green triangular folds of husk
until she can sprinkle the black ash
of seeds onto the clay.
Here she buries each daughter sin,
tiny black communion wafers
riven, rotting, fecund.

Above her hangs the cross of a tree.
The chapel of her childhood.
Each silver underbelly of its leaves, rings
maple, maple, maple
until she can feel the embrace of roots,
buried limbs beneath her knees,
and she sinks, digs deeper
until each nail on her right hand is black,
an omega and an origin.

III.
When I was a child I believed in the music of
my father's voice rising along the ladder
of his bones, my own ear pressed hard
against his chest. His voice, god-sized, holy.
Now when I hear my grown son sing,
that same myth rises, a stone tossed
into the river of a crowd,
concentric sound staining the air,

until guitar strings turn trumpet,
and *John the Revelator* rides into the room,
fills all our hands with clapping song
and a new heaven descends
onto the old wood stage on Beale Street
in the heart of Memphis.

IV.
Poetry is the deep listening
to a silence which is no silence
in the ear of a deaf child who can hear
the crackling of a canna into bloom.
A young man I know tells me
some days his deaf sister was so weak
they would sign into her hand,
into the inner ear of her palm.
Music is this synesthesia of absence
and plenty. The pure mind praying
where nothing is asked for.
And this nothing heals.

V.
When I read the Book of Genesis, I want
to build a different story where
Blue Adam and Blue Eve create,
out of the imagination, a garden that lasts
in the concentric lives
of the children they will bear.

Let there be the raw beauty of wilderness.
Let the Tree of Life and the Tree which is the Rood
bleed nothing more than sweet apples.
Let forgiveness be an oblivion.
And let jewel-colored horses, unbridled, without riders,
stand up on hind feet,
raise their voices to the clouds.

Notes

Pages 1 & 8: "City that ripens on the tree of the world" is a line from Maga-
dalena Tulli's novel *Dreams and Stones* translated from the Polish by Bill John-
ston (Archipelago Press, 2004).

Page 10: Stanisław Wyspiański (1869-1907), a painter of the Art Nouveau
movement in Poland and a colleague of Józef Mehoffer (1869-1946).

Page 11: Jordan Park was established in 1889 as the first public park and
children's playground in Kraków. The first of its kind in Europe, it was devel-
oped by Dr. Henryk Jordan (1842-1907), a Polish physician and professor at
the Jagiellonian University. Jordan was a pioneer of physical education who
popularized the idea of public landscapes for physical exercise. This poem
refers to the circular labyrinth of hornbeam trees at the park's center where
45 busts of famous Poles, commissioned by Dr. Jordan in 1907 and created
by sculptors Alfred Daun and Michal Korpal, were displayed. During World
World II, the park was destroyed, with the exception of 22 of the busts and a
monument of Dr. Jordan. The park has since been re-established and enlarged
to 52 acres to include various outdoor sports venues.

Page 11: *Pani* is the formal, respectful second person pronoun "you" in Polish
used when speaking to or of a woman.

Page 15: From Andrew Marvell's poem "The Garden."

Page 17: *God sent me to the sea for pearls* is a line from one of John Clare's asy-
lum poems written after his psychological collapse in 1837.

Page 25: "In the heart's cellar, sleepless" appears in Ingeborg Bachmann's
poem "Autumn Maneuver" translated from the German by Peter Filkin and
published in *Songs in Flight: The Collected Poems* (Marsilio Publishers, 1994).

Page 28: Lwów was founded in 1256 C.E. and remained a part of Polish territory through much of the early twentieth century. During World War II, the city was seized by the Soviets in 1939 and renamed Lvov. From 1941 to 1944 the city was occupied by the Nazis who created the Lvov (or Lemberg) Ghetto, housing about 120,000 Jews nearly all of whom were exterminated. Simon Wiesenthal, famous Nazi hunter, was one of the few who survived. In 1945, Lvov became part of the Ukraine under Soviet rule, and was renamed Lviv in 1991 when the Ukraine achieved independence from the USSR.

Page 33: Józef Mehoffer (1869-1946), painter of the Art Nouveau movement in Poland and a colleague of Stanisław Wyspiański (1869-1907).

Page 34: *Make me a stone—the heart of a stone* is a line from *With the Skin: The Poems of Aleksandr Wat* translated from the Polish by Czesław Miłosz and Leonard Nathan.

Page 41: A line from a partial sonnet written in the 1520's which reads: "Blessed is the soul where time does not run; through you it is formed to contemplate God." (*The Selected Poems of Michelangelo* translated from the Italian by Christopher Ryan.)

Page 49: "If Grief Were a Bird" is the title of a poem appearing in Susan Wood's collection *the book of ten* (University of Pittsburgh Press, 2011).

Page 51: The serinette was a small organ made at Mirecourt in the Vosges region of France and used in parlors from the beginning of the 18th century to teach small songbirds such as canaries to sing. Eavan Boland uses this instrument metaphorically to discuss the role of the lyric in contemporary poetry in her essay "The Serinette Principle" published in *Parnassus Poetry Review* (1993).

Page 58: *A wise man loves water* is an aphorism attributed to Confucius.

Page 61: *Oświęcim* is the name of the Polish town that became the site of the German death camp *Auschwitz-Birkenau*.

Page 64: Kazimierz is the former Jewish quarter of Kraków, Poland, dating from the 14th century until World War II.

Page 68: *Roslein, Roslein, Roslein* is a partial line from Goethe's poem "Heiden-roslein" ("Rosebud in the Heather") published in 1771. The poem concerns lost virginity and is a dialogue between an urchin boy and a rosebud he finds, plucks from the heather.

Page 68: *Giedd* in Old English means *song* or *poem*, and appears in the final line of "Wulf and Eadwacer" (translated as "Wolf and Wealthwatcher"), an Old English poem in which the female speaker laments her exile and that of the man she loves. The poem implies that she is both responsible for and a victim of this exile which concerns rivalry between the two men of the poem's title. The final line, "uncer giedd geador" ("our song together") implies that the "giedd" they have made is a child. This is one of the few Anglo-Saxon poems spoken by a woman.

The Richard Snyder Publication Series

This book is the sixteenth in a series honoring the memory of Richard Snyder (1925-1986), poet, fiction writer, playwright and longtime professor of English at Ashland University. Snyder served for fifteen years as English Department chair and was co-founder (in 1969) and co-editor of the Ashland Poetry Press. He was also co-founder of the Creative Writing major at the school, one of the first on the undergraduate level in the country. In selecting the manuscript for this book, the editors kept in mind Snyder's tenacious dedication to craftsmanship and thematic integrity.

Deborah Fleming, Editor, selected finalists for the 2012 contest.
Final judge: Elizabeth Spires.

Snyder Award Winners:

1997: Wendy Battin for *Little Apocalypse*

1998: David Ray for *Demons in the Diner*

1999: Philip Brady for *Weal*

2000: Jan Lee Ande for *Instructions for Walking on Water*

2001: Corrinne Clegg Hales for *Separate Escapes*

2002: Carol Barrett for *Calling in the Bones*

2003: Vern Rutsala for *The Moment's Equation*

2004: Christine Gelineau for *Remorseless Loyalty*

2005: Benjamin S. Grossberg for *Underwater Lengths in a Single Breath*

2006: Lorna Knowles Blake for *Permanent Address*

2007: Helen Pruitt Wallace for *Shimming the Glass House*

2008: Marc J. Sheehan for *Vengeful Hymns*

2009: Jason Schneiderman for *Striking Surface*

2010: Mary Makofske for *Traction*

2011: Gabriel Spera for *The Rigid Body*

2012: Robin Davidson for *Luminous Other*